SANCTUARY

The Story of Three Arch Rocks

To Brett, who was with me every mile.

I wish to extend my gratitude to Worth Mathewson, the Oregon Historical Society, and the Tillamook County Pioneer Museum for assisting me in my research. I give special thanks to Roy W. Lowe with the U.S. Department of the Interior's Fish and Wildlife Service, who answered my many questions and unselfishly took the time to explain current efforts to save the animals of Three Arch Rocks.

Many of the details concerning Finley and Bohlman's visits to Three Arch Rocks come from *Sanctuary! Sanctuary!* written by Finley's friend Dallas Lore Sharp, and from *William L. Finley, Pioneer Wildlife Photographer,* written by Worth Mathewson. Additional information is derived from my own trip to Oceanside to view the refuge. Quotations from Finley's writings on pages 4, 10, 17, and 18 are taken from Mathewson.

Special permission to reproduce Finley and Bohlman's photographs (negative numbers A2517, A2519, A2471, A2464) was granted by the Oregon Historical Society. All other nature sketches and illustrations are my own.

Henry Holt and Company, Inc. / *Publishers since 1866*
115 West 18th Street / New York, New York 10011

Henry Holt is a registered
trademark of Henry Holt and Company, Inc.

Published in Canada by Fitzhenry & Whiteside Ltd.,
195 Allstate Parkway, Markham, Ontario L3R 4T8.

Library of Congress Cataloging-in-Publication Data
Fraser, Mary Ann.
    Sanctuary, the story of Three Arch Rocks /
written and illustrated by Mary Ann Fraser.
    1. Wildlife conservation—Oregon—Three Arch Rocks—Juvenile
literature.   2. Finley, William L. (William Lovell), 1876–1953—
Journeys—Juvenile literature.   3. Bohlman, Herman—Journeys—
Juvenile literature.   4. Three Arch Rocks (Or.)—Juvenile
literature.   [1. Three Arch Rocks (Or.)   2. Wildlife refuges.
3. Wildlife conservation.   4. Finley, William L. (William Lovell),
1876–1953.   5. Bohlman, Herman.]   I. Title.
    SK439.F73   1994   333.95′16′0979544—dc20   93-41362

ISBN 0-8050-2920-6

First Edition—1994

Printed in the United State of America on acid-free paper.∞
10 9 8 7 6 5 4 3 2 1

The illustrations for this book were done in acrylic on watercolor paper.

SANCTUARY

The Story of Three Arch Rocks

Written and illustrated by
Mary Ann Fraser

Henry Holt and Company
New York

William L. Finley

Herman Bohlman

Half a mile out to sea, sportsmen aboard a small tugboat were firing at will toward three sea-swept rocks. On shore, William Finley and Herman Bohlman could not believe their eyes. The two young photographers saw thousands of birds screeching and circling their eggs and chicks. Sea lions and seals were racing to the sea, churning the surf with their frenzied dives. But the defenseless birds and seals that clung to the small islands known as Three Arch Rocks could not escape. When at last the tug steamed away, it left behind hundreds of dead and wounded animals struggling or floating in the surf.

Finley wrote, "The beaches at Oceanside were littered with dead birds following the Sunday carnage."

William and Herman had come in June of 1901 to the Oregon coast at Oceanside to photograph birds, especially the seabirds that clouded the air, dotted the ocean, and smothered the basalt crags of Three Arch Rocks.

Two or three times a week they saw hunters row to the rocks to kill the huge but slow-moving sea lions for their skins and oil. Panicked by the blasting guns, the sea lions would stampede into the water, often crushing their newborn pups. For the two birdwatchers, though, the sportsmen who came to the rocks each Sunday for target practice were even worse. These gunmen were not killing the animals for food, feathers, or fur—they were doing it just for sport.

By the end of the summer, when they returned to Portland, William and Herman realized that the animal colonies could not survive much longer. The birds and marine mammals needed help—and quickly. The young photographers felt that if they didn't take some action, no one would. They vowed to make the difficult journey to Three Arch Rocks, and to put an end to the slaughter, as soon as possible.

Fig.1 Harbor Seal

Fig.2 California Sea Lion

Stellar Sea Lion Fig.3

A VERY
STYLISH HAT

No. 25677
This fine Milan straw hat is trimmed on
the left side with four Amazon parrot
wings, decorated with a beautiful bow,
and finished with a dotted veil.
Each...$3.95

Finley and Bohlman kept their promise. They returned in June of 1903 to study and document the wildlife of Three Arch Rocks. By now, both were in their late twenties. They had met as boys while watching birds on the streets of Portland, Oregon. Although William was more outgoing and talkative than Herman, they soon became good friends.

Like other early naturalists, William and Herman had killed birds and gathered eggs for private collections and museums, and had also provided feathers for milliners to make women's hat decorations. But even before coming to Three Arch Rocks the two collectors had realized they were destroying the very animals they cared about most. So instead of killing bird specimens with guns, they began shooting them with cameras. This new approach to preserving wildlife made them pioneers in conservation.

Unable to persuade someone to take them to the rocks, the determined young men lugged a small boat called a dory and all of their supplies, including food, a tent, fresh water, fuel, clothing, and photographic equipment to the beach at Oceanside. But as they arrived on shore their hopes of leaving immediately for the rocks vanished. A dense curtain of fog extended from the coastal mountains out over Three Arch Rocks. Its moisture clung to Herman's thick mustache as he watched wild breakers batter the shoreline.

All day William and Herman paced up and down the beach, anxiously looking for a break in the triple sets of pounding waves so they could launch their boat. As night approached, they set up camp. Suddenly the clouds let loose with a downpour. Hunching beneath his wide-brimmed hat, William dashed into the leaky tent, followed by Herman. They would have to wait for clear weather and calmer seas.

Day after day torrential rain seeped through the canvas tent, soaking their bedding and clothes. At times they must have wanted to quit and return home. But watching the gulls soar above the crags and the clownlike puffins plunge into the surf to feed helped remind them of their goal.

After sixteen days of storms, fog, and rough seas, William and Herman lost patience. They decided to chance the crossing in two trips. They packed the first half of their heavy supplies and fragile equipment into the fourteen-foot dory and launched it into the waves.

Their little craft plowed over the first breaker and crashed down its other side. It rose and paused on the crest of the next wave, then shot into a deep trough. Leaping up the next green wall, the boat reached the curling peak of the third wave just as it combed. CRASH! Half a ton of foamy water struck the rowers, flipping their boat. Another wave picked up the dory and tossed it empty onto the beach. William and Herman spent the rest of the day scurrying along the shore to gather and dry their supplies.

The next day the young men again headed into the waves. Once more a wall of water swamped their boat, further damaging their delicate camera equipment.

"We reached a sort of amphibious state, where a condition of water soak was normal."

Finally, on their nineteenth day on the desolate shore, William and Herman saw the first true signs of clear weather. The anxious adventurers charged into the now-lower surf for the third time. Their boat rose and fell over each swell like a roller-coaster. At last, it passed the breakers and coasted through smooth water.

After rowing half a mile, the men reached the three main rocks, each of which featured a wave-cut arch the size of a small ship. Nowhere on the first or second rocks could they find a place to land their dory. The high and wild waves tossed them about like driftwood.

Carefully they navigated around the third rock, Shag. If they could not find a port they would have to give up their mission and return to shore. Rounding the island's point, they found a small cove. Riding in close on the crest of a wave, they slung their supplies on to a dry ledge, hoping their equipment wouldn't slide into the water.

Wasting no time, they rowed hard back to the beach for the rest of their cargo. They could only hope that the rising tide would not wash their precious supplies off of Shag.

Fig. 1

Double-crested Cormorant

Pelagic Cormorant

Fig. 2

CORMORANTS
There are three species of cormorants, or shags, that nest on the Oregon coast: the double-crested cormorant, the Brandt's cormorant, and the pelagic cormorant. Each species builds its own kind of nest. Unlike other birds, cormorants have feathers that get wet. That is why they are often seen standing on a rock or piling with their wings outstretched to dry. They feed mostly on fish, which they catch by diving as deep as 180 feet and swimming with their feet.

Once again Herman and William maneuvered through the breakers. Finally, when the remaining gear was on Shag, they waited for an especially powerful wave and rowed in with its trough. Herman made a flying leap at a mussel-encrusted ledge. Then William rowed in again and threw his friend a rope with a block and tackle so he could pull the boat onto the craggy rocks before it was smashed to pieces by the surf.

Looking about for a place to stow their dory, they spied a bull sea lion the size of a large bear sprawled across an ideal shelf about ten feet above their heads. Waving their arms and yelling, they drove the annoyed beast off its ledge and stood back as it plunged into the heaving sea.

NORTHERN (STELLER) SEA LION
This endangered marine mammal is the largest sea lion. The males, or bulls, are larger than any bear when full grown. The females, or cows, are one-third the size of the males. During rough weather these sea lions stay in the water. Otherwise, they are usually found sleeping on rocky shores. They feed at night on fish, squid, clams, and crabs.

Their dory was now safe and secure, but where would they sleep? Luckily they found a weathered rift barely wide enough to hold them. Herman chipped at the rock with an axe and chisel while William pried loose pieces of basalt to enlarge the space a little. With the tent supported by the dory's oars, their camp was ready for the night.

Although the men were exhausted, they found it hard to sleep. Not only was their campsite cramped, it was noisy. Waves blasted into the caverns and rocky arches, thundering like cannons. Thousands of nesting birds performed a never-ending symphony of wing beating, bill clacking, and screeching, accompanied by the bellows and barks of sea lions and harbor seals. And the constant whistling wind could not blow away the odor of briny sea air and piles of bird guano.

Herman and William had to be careful not to toss or turn in their sleep. A move too far to one side would mean a fall off the precipice onto a lumbering sea lion or, worse, into the icy surf forty feet below.

WESTERN GULL
The western gull is the largest and darkest of all Pacific coast gulls. It usually lays between two and four eggs. Once the chicks hatch, they quickly learn to peck at the red mark on their parent's bill. This causes the adult to regurgitate its food for the chick to eat.

"Looking for a camping spot on the rough side of the cliff was a good deal like hunting for a lodging on a winding staircase...."

As the morning light struck the sea-worn cliffs, William and Herman began their work on Three Arch Rocks. The isolated slopes, crevices, and ledges provide ideal nesting places for seabirds, which reproduce slowly. But these conditions also made the naturalists' task more difficult.

As the men scaled the two-hundred-foot rock wall that rose above their tent, they tried hard not to disturb the clusters of birds sitting on eggs or raising their young. Everywhere, cormorant nests were stuccoed to the outcroppings. Common murres, which don't use a nest, had placed their pear-shaped eggs on the narrow ledges that the climbers needed for footholds. Meanwhile, screeching gulls, protecting their chicks, dove at the intruders. Just as William or Herman would get close enough for a photograph, either one would accidentally bang the camera's awkward tripod against a rock, scaring off the birds.

"We awoke the next morning feeling as if we had spent the night on top of a broken picket fence."

COMMON MURRE
The adult common murre fishes far away from land and returns only for nesting. The parents share incubation of their single pear-shaped egg, which rests either on a narrow ledge or on top of its parent's webbed feet. Murre chicks are fed for 18 to 25 days in the colony. Then they leap off the cliffs into the sea to migrate north with their fathers.

In 1903, cameras were large and bulky, and negatives had to be made on chemically treated glass plates that cracked easily. The men had to lug all this equipment up and down the steep cliffs, which were slippery from ocean spray and bird droppings. One false step could mean serious injury, or even death.

Although their work was dangerous, both men enjoyed what they were doing. Sometimes they photographed each other in funny situations, or used a string attached to the camera's shutter to take pictures of themselves on the sheer cliffs.

PIGEON GUILLEMOT
These very noisy birds, which have a high thin whistle, are named for their pigeonlike size. Similar to puffins, they use their wings to "fly" underwater when chasing fish and other small sea creatures. Pairs incubate their eggs for thirty days in nests placed ten to forty feet above the water.

Shag's steep and jagged south side was barren except for the gull, murre, and cormorant nests. Its more shaded north side had some plant growth and, in places, bird droppings covered its slope to a depth of three to four feet. Tufted puffins burrowed into this guano and the soil to make their nests. Storm-petrels also dug into the slope to make their homes. While one of the parents sat on the nest, the other would fly far out to sea, returning only after sunset to avoid predators.

STORM-PETREL
The fork-tailed storm-petrel is one of the smallest seabirds.

Herman and William knew that few people had studied the storm-petrel's nesting habits. So for one night they climbed to the top of Shag. Afraid they might slide over the edge if they dozed off, they anchored themselves between two rocks. There they stayed awake all night, listening and watching as the returning storm-petrels fluttered home, twittering to their waiting mates.

TUFTED PUFFIN
The puffin's bill becomes very colorful during breeding season, which is why it has been nicknamed the "clown of the sea" or "sea parrot." Since this bird has small wings, it launches off steep coastal slopes into the air, using the wind to gain speed for flight. With its bill and feet, the puffin carves a tunnel into the grassy slope for its nest. Puffin chicks eat fish and squid brought back to the nest by their parents. The birds "fly" underwater by beating their small finlike wings, while spines on their tongue and on the roof of their mouth help them hold slippery fish.

Fig. 2

Fig. 1

TUFTED PUFFIN

After William and Herman had spent fourteen days clinging to the rocks like barnacles to a ship's hull, their film, food, and water were gone. They loaded their dory with their valuable cargo of glass negatives and notes and launched it into a large cresting wave. Herds of sea lions bellowed and flocks of ocean birds filled the sky overhead. Migrating gray whales, which had stopped to feed around the rocks, spouted misty fountains and slapped their tails on the water's surface.

William and Herman had been the first humans to camp on the rocks. They must have wondered, as they rowed to shore, if their work would make a difference. Could two young men stop boatloads of sportsmen and hunters? They knew that President Roosevelt relied on naturalists in the field to suggest sites in need of protection, but would their few pictures convince him to take action?

A few months later William traveled across the country to Washington, D.C., to meet with Theodore Roosevelt. At the White House, he was ushered into a room where the President would hear the story of Three Arch Rocks. The large door swung shut with a thud, and William stood face-to-face with the smiling, burly figure of the President. All of the young naturalists' hard work came down to this moment.

William spread the photographs on a table and told the President about the wondrous creatures that lived on the rocks, and the hunters and sportsmen who were wiping them out. He explained how a wildlife refuge could ensure that these seabirds and marine mammals would be around for future generations to enjoy.

The President's eyes widened. "Bully, bully," he exclaimed as he pounded his fists on the table. "We'll make a sanctuary out of Three Arch Rocks."

But William's job was not over. For four years he had to lobby hard to make sure the President delivered on his promise. While waiting for Washington to act, William and Herman, together with the Oregon Audubon Society, worked to establish the State Model Bird Law that would outlaw sport shooting of seabirds. Once the law was passed, they contacted the Oregon state game warden, who, armed with the new law, confronted the tugboat owner and put a stop to the shooting trips to Three Arch Rocks.

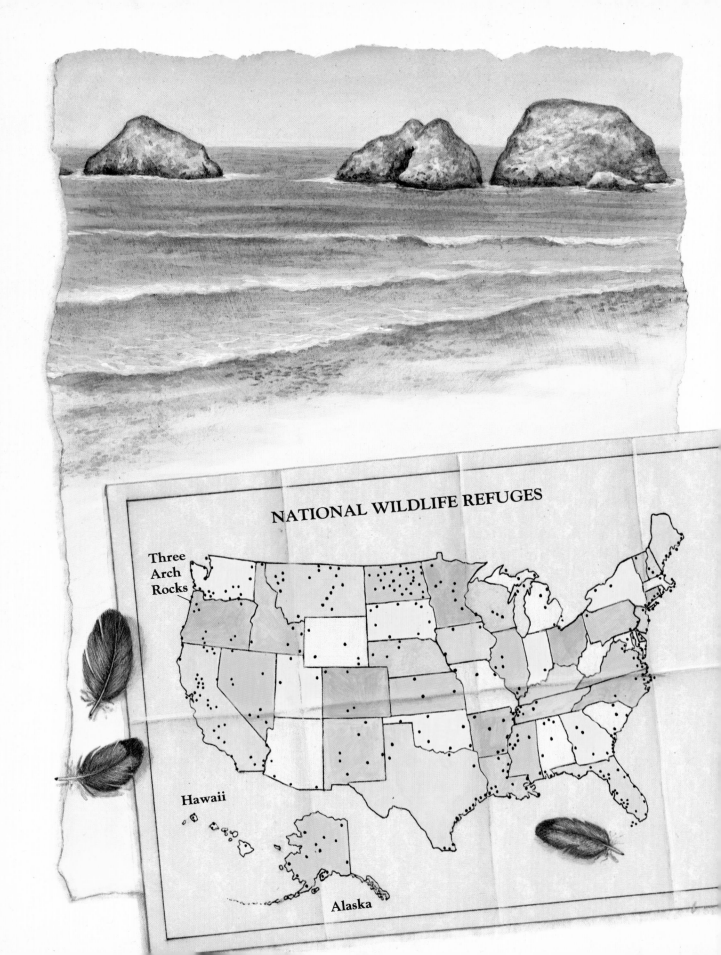

NATIONAL WILDLIFE REFUGES

Three
Arch
Rocks

Hawaii

Alaska

On October 14, 1907, by Executive Order, President Roosevelt declared Three Arch Rocks a National Wildlife Refuge. It was America's third sanctuary and the first ever on the West Coast. Today it is one of almost 500 such refuges administered by the U.S. Fish and Wildlife Service. The rocks offer protection to thirteen species of birds and three species of pinnipeds (seals and sea lions), including the northern (Steller) sea lion, the Aleutian race of the Canada goose, the peregrine falcon, the bald eagle, and the California subspecies of the brown pelican, which are listed as threatened or endangered species. Visitors to Three Arch Rocks can view the animals, but from at least 500 feet away and preferably from shore.

Despite federal protection, people are still disturbing the nesting birds. Boaters, divers, jet skiers, and airplane pilots continue to come too close to the rocks. Fortunately, concerned individuals are working for change through education and new restrictions.

But Three Arch Rocks is only one part of a much larger ecosystem. Natural disasters, overfishing, oil spills, and pollution that occur thousands of miles away are taking their toll on the animals that come to these rocks. In June 1993, for example, a combination of weather cycles and oil slicks reduced the nesting common murre population from 250,000 birds to just 260.

William Finley and Herman Bohlman risked their lives and reputations to change what they knew to be wrong. We all observe the world around us. And we, too, can sound the alarm when our natural world is threatened, and work to protect it.

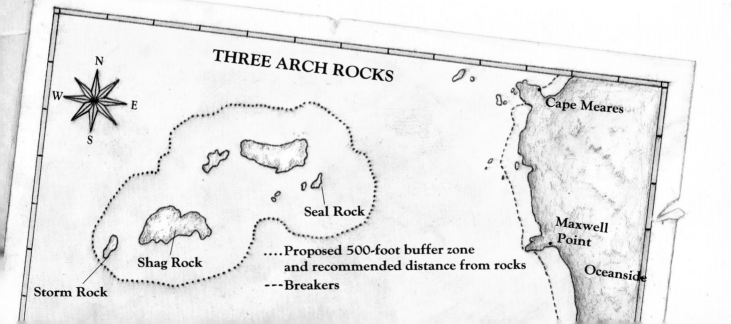

What Can We Do?

Throughout the world, young people are becoming important protectors of our natural resources. In Comer, Georgia, schoolchildren wrote to their governor and the newspapers when their local state park was about to shut down owing to a lack of funds. The kids saved Watson Mill Bridge State Park and the animals and plants that live there. Sixth-grade students at Flowing Wells Junior High School in Tucson, Arizona, are raising endangered desert pupfish in ponds on the school grounds. And Kids FACE, an environmental organization started by nine-year-old Melissa Poe, now has over 30,000 members in clubs around the world.

If you want to learn more about the environment and how to protect it, or you want to start an organization of your own, here are some groups that can help. Which one interests you?

Center for Marine Conservation
1725 DeSales Street, NW, Ste. 500
Washington, DC 20036
The center is a nonprofit membership organization dedicated to protecting marine wildlife and their resources. Educational materials are available.

Children for Old Growth
P.O. Box 1090
Redway, CA 95560
When you join this organization dedicated to saving old forests you receive a large forest poster and a newsletter written by kids.

Children's Alliance for Protection
   of the Environment (CAPE)
P.O. Box 307
Austin, TX 78767
CAPE is an international organization that offers information about kids' projects to protect the environment and how you can join them. The group publishes a newsletter written by and for children, called "MANY HANDS."

Children's Rainforest
P.O. Box 936
Lewiston, ME 04240
This is a children's group working to protect the Costa Rican rainforest.

Environmental Youth Alliance
P.O. Box 34097, Station D
Vancouver BC, V6J 4M1 Canada
This group is involved in many issues, including preserving old-growth forests.

FOWL, Friends of Wild Life
P.O. Box 477
Petaluma, CA 94953
For a self-addressed stamped envelope, this group will send you information on starting a wildlife club in your own area.

Humane Society of the United States
Youth Education Division
67 Salem Road
East Haddam, CT 06423-0362
The Humane Society has a large educational program for children and offers many publications. Its student action guide is full of useful ideas for things kids can do.

Kids Against Pollution (KAP)
Tenakill School
275 High Street
Closter, NJ 07624
Started by elementary-school children, this group is for kids of all ages. Membership is $6 and gets you a packet of information on stopping pollution and news about other KAP kids.

Kids for a Clean Environment (Kids FACE)
P.O. Box 158254
Nashville, TN 37215
This organization was started by nine-year-old Melissa Poe and offers free membership. Members receive a bimonthly newsletter called "Kids FACE."

Kids for Saving Earth (KSE)
P.O. Box 47247
Plymouth, MN 55447-0247
Sponsored by Target Stores, this group's purpose is to educate kids on ways they can protect the environment. They have a newsletter and can send you a packet on starting your own environmental group.

Kids Network
National Geographic Society
Educational Services, Dept. 1001
Washington, D.C. 20077
Kids Network is a telecommunications system that allows the sharing of environmental information. It also offers materials and publications.

Kids Save the Planet! (Kids STOP)
P.O. Box 471
Forest Hills, NY 11375
This group was started by a seven-year-old. If you send $2 with a self-addressed stamped envelope, they will send you a packet on starting and running a project of your own.

National Audubon Society
700 Broadway
New York, NY 10003
The National Audubon Society's mission is to create wise public policy regarding wildlife and habitats. It provides educational materials, teacher aids, a classroom sponsorship program, and membership.

National Wildlife Federation
1412 Sixteenth Street, NW
Washington, DC 20036-2266
The National Wildlife Federation is an environmental group working with federal and state governments to get them to protect our natural resources. Publications for children, leadership training, camps, educational materials, magazines for all ages, and membership are all available through this organization.

U.S. Department of the Interior
Fish and Wildlife Service
Washington, DC 20240
This service is the nation's principal conservation agency and manages the National Wildlife Refuge System. A volunteer program and publications are available to interested individuals.

U.S. Environmental Protection Agency
Public Information Center
401 M Street, SW
Washington, DC 20460
This agency is designed to provide federal environmental regulatory and educational information, which includes the annual President's Environmental Youth Awards as well as elementary and secondary student kits.

All addresses have been confirmed, but organizations do move, change names, and close down. We have omitted phone numbers because they change even more frequently. A call to Information, or a query letter, will give you the most current address and phone number.

GLOSSARY

basalt: a hard, dark rock of volcanic origin

block and tackle: a pulley block and ropes used for lifting and hauling heavy objects

conservation: the protection of natural resources from waste, loss, or harm

dory: a small, narrow, flat-bottomed fishing boat

ecosystem: a community of living things and their environment

guano: bird or bat droppings

habitat: an area where certain types of animals occur

pinniped: mammal that lives in the water and has flippers; includes seals, sea lions, and walruses

refuge: a protection or shelter from harm

rift: a narrow crack in a rock

sanctuary: a reserved area for animals and birds to protect them from hunting and disturbances

shag: another name for a cormorant

trough: the long, narrow hollow between two waves

Western Gull

Fork-tailed
Storm-Petrel

Leach's
Storm-Petrel

Flat
Ground

Burrow

Common
Murre

Tufted
Puffin

Double-
crested
Cormorant

Cliff Ledge

Brandt's
Cormorant

Cliff

Pelagic
Cormorant

Rock Crevice

California
Sea Lion

Pigeon
Guillemot

Boulders

Brown
Pelican